Nine Steps To Becoming A Better Lector

Nick Wagner

Resource Publi
San Jose, Calif

Reprint Department
Resource Publications, Inc.
160 E. Virginia Street #290
San Jose, CA 95112-5876
1-408-286-8505 (voice)
1-408-287-8748 (fax)

Library of Congress Cataloging-in-Publication Data
Wagner, Nick, 1957
   Nine steps to becoming a better lector / Nick Wagner.
     p. cm.
   Includes bibliographical references.
   ISBN 0-89390-503-8 (pbk.)
   1. Lay readers. I. Title.
   BV677. W34 2000
   264'.64--dc21   00-020961

00 01 02 03 04 | 5 4 3 2 1

Editorial director: Nick Wagner
Production coordinator: Mike Sagara
Copyeditor: Robin Witkin
Illustrations: George Collopy, Mike Sagara

CONTENTS

PREFACE

I became a lector when I was seventeen years old. I wish I could say I had done so because I felt a call from the Lord or because I felt a keen desire to evangelize those who had not yet heard the word or some such lofty, spiritual motivation.

The truth is, I liked the attention. When I walked up to the ambo, all the eyes in the church were focused on me. Perhaps this is not the best reason to become a lector, but it is the reason that a lot of us got started and the reason some of us are still doing it after many years. I used to feel a little guilty about my less-than-pure motivation until I realized that God can use even my weaknesses to accomplish God's goals. I began to accept that I would never be visited by winged angels bearing burning coals to purify my lips. I would never see a vision or hear a voice or receive written instructions from the Lord directing the exact way in which I was supposed to live out my baptismal commitment. My call was in fact my selfish desire for attention.

What has helped me reconcile my selfishness with the mandate to be selfless and to sacrifice myself, a mandate I proclaim almost every time I read, is a commitment I made early on to continually improve my skills as a lector. If I am going to *take* attention from the community, I feel obligated to *give* my best effort back to them when I read.

I thought I was a "good enough" lector almost from the time I started. I could be heard clearly, and I used pretty good eye contact. Isn't that all that's expected of a lector? But the more I proclaimed the Scriptures, the more I realized there is never really a "good enough" minister. All the Scriptures point to the paschal mystery—Christ's self-sacrifice for us. The more I read, the more I understood that God wasn't calling me just to be a good lector. God was and is calling me to sacrifice myself for the sake of the community, just as Christ did.

Every lector has to master some basics just to be "good enough." However, once those basics are mastered, every lector is faced with a choice. Am I going to be satisfied with "good enough," or am I going to challenge and stretch myself for the sake of the community? Am I going to work to become a better lector next year than I was last year? Am I going to go out of my way to learn new ways to proclaim God's word more powerfully?

I would respectfully suggest that neither God nor the church needs lectors who are "good enough." What we need are lectors who will sacrifice themselves. What we need are lectors who will work every week to give back to the community more than they take from it. What we need are lectors who are driven to give their best effort—plus a little bit more—in order to proclaim the paschal mystery.

You are that kind of lector or you wouldn't be reading this book. It is my hope that some of the techniques you find here will help you in your continuous efforts to improve and extend yourself. For some of you, these nine steps will be reminders and encouragements of some of the things you already do to prepare. For others, some of these steps may seem overwhelming and challenging. Keep in mind that your goal isn't to be the best lector God has ever created. It is to be a little better next time than you were last time. Work in small but consistent doses to improve your skills. If you can do that, you will be meeting the Gospel's mandate to self-sacrifice.

May the Lord be on your lips and in your hearts so that you may worthily proclaim God's word.

Solemnity of Christ the King
The last Sunday of the second millennium

Sculptors of the silence

Lectors must first be silent. This seems paradoxical until we recall the story of Elijah. We encounter Elijah in the lectionary (Nineteenth Sunday of Ordinary Time, Cycle A) at a time when he fears for his life. But do we recall how he got to that point?

Elijah, a prophet of the Lord God, had set up a contest with the prophets of Baal, the pagan god (cf. 1 Kings 18). He proposed they both build up a stack of firewood and each place half of a bull on the wood to be burned as a sacrifice. Elijah then challenged the prophets of Baal to call on their god to light the fire and he agreed to do the same. No matter how hard they tried, the prophets of Baal were unable to get their god to light the fire. They called on Baal from morning to noon and throughout the afternoon, but no answer.

When it was Elijah's turn, he upped the ante. He dug a trench around his sacrifice and had the people pour twelve urns of water over it, so much that the water filled up the trench. Then he called upon the Lord God to ignite the soggy wood. God not only lit the fire; the fire consumed the bull, the wood, the stones on which the wood rested, the dust around the stones, and all the water in the trench. Then, in his zeal, Elijah called upon the people to murder the prophets of Baal. Pretty much a full day's work. Elijah must have been feeling pretty good about himself.

Until the queen found out. Queen Jezebel didn't like it that all her court prophets had been killed off. So she sent the troops out to slay Elijah. Even though he had just witnessed how powerful God was, Elijah went and hid in the desert. He then fell into despair and prayed for the Lord to take his life. An angel came and told him to go to the mountain of God, Horeb, and wait there for the Lord. And that's where we find him in the lectionary reading.

Elijah is waiting in a cave on the mountain for God. A voice comes to him and asks, "What are you doing here, Elijah?" Elijah answers in his despair that he fears for his life. He is told to go and stand on the mountain. Soon a raging wind with the power to crush rocks goes by. But God is not in the wind. After the wind comes an earthquake. But God is not in the earthquake. Then there is a fire. But God is not in the fire. Then comes "a sound of sheer silence" (1 Kings 19:12; NRSV). And in that sheer silence is where Elijah hears God's voice.

Elijah was a prophet who was used to powerful signs from God. But in the end, when his life depended on it, he could not find God in any of the big and powerful ways we might expect to find God. When Elijah needed God most, God's voice was in the silence.

This is true for lots of people, and perhaps it is true for you. God more often speaks to us in the silent moments than in big, powerful, overwhelming ways. And if this is true for lots of people, we have quite a challenge before us as lectors. If God speaks in silence, how dare we break that silence?

Breaking the silence is an awesome responsibility. I sometimes think of it as the responsibility a sculptor has when faced with a fine block of natural marble. The stone itself is beautiful. In fact, it would be extremely difficult for most people to make it more beautiful. And yet, there are some artists among us who can take that beautiful stone and shape it into something even more meaningful and more graceful than its natural, God-given shape.

As lectors, we are artists, sculptors of the silence. Our craft is to find the voice of God in the sheer silence and then, using our words as sculptors use their tools, to chisel and shape the silence into the proclaimed word of God. Like sculptors, we need to be careful not to slip, not to chip off too much, not to work haphazardly, lest we damage the work. We hone our craft and discipline ourselves in our art so the word will take shape in our assemblies each time we dare to break the silence.

Pray

The question that was put to Elijah as he waited in the cave was, "What are you doing here?" What Elijah was doing was praying. Praying with all his mind and heart that somehow God would become present to him, that somehow, God's word would become known to him.

It may seem unnecessary to exhort lectors to pray. How many of us, knees shaking, have approached the ambo reciting a fervent prayer that we would not mispronounce the string of ancient and unpronounceable names in the reading that was our bad luck to draw on some given week? But this is not the type of prayer that should be the first priority in our ministry. We need to focus on a deeper, truer type of prayer. Instead of prayer that is focused on asking God for things, we need to understand that prayer is first of all *listening.*

True prayer is a paradox because we cannot pray until we admit "we do not know how to pray as we ought" (Rom 8:26). Prayer is a gift from God. According to the *Catechism of the Catholic Church*, "Prayer is the response of faith to the free promise of salvation and also a response of love to the thirst of the only Son of God" (2561).

For the Christian, and especially for lectors, prayer is the daily habit of being in the presence of and in communion with (listening to) our loving God whose word we proclaim. We are all called to this communion through prayer. The stories we read on Sunday remind us that God has called us to prayer from our earliest times. Abraham offered his son in prayerful sacrifice to the Lord (Gen 22:1–19); Moses beseeches the Lord to have mercy on his people (Ex 32:1–34:9); David, the shepherd king, prays for his people and in their name (2 Sam 7:18–29). Using Elijah as an example, James tells us, "The prayer of the righteous is powerful and effective" (5:16b–18, NRSV); and the Psalms are the "masterwork of prayer in the Old Testament" (CCC 2585).

For Christians, Jesus is the paradigm of prayer. Jesus teaches us to pray both by example and by explicit instruction. Jesus instructs us that true prayer must mean a heart filled with faith and love (cf. Mt 5:23–24,44–45; 6:7,14–15,21,25,33). Jesus gives us the gift of the Lord's Prayer in response to the disciples' request, "Lord, teach us to pray" (Lk 11:1, NRSV; cf. Mt 6:9–13).

God has always called people to prayer—to listening—but it is with Abraham that we first begin to understand how prayer makes us able to hear God's word (cf. CCC 2570 ff.). Abraham is completely open to God's will and has his heart set on doing exactly what God asks of him. He is first of all a listener. Even when Abraham is asked to sacrifice his son, his gift from God in fulfillment of the covenant, his faith remains strong. Abraham is the antithesis of Adam who did not listen to God and did not do God's will. Abraham's faithfulness in prayer once again forms all humanity into God's likeness and restores us to the time before Adam's sin. Prayer re-makes us into God's image.

In order to pray, we need to be disciplined. To be disciplined is to be a disciple—to form ourselves in an art form or a way of living or thinking. A disciple of a great musician will spend hours listening to and imitating his or her master. A lector must be a disciple of the word—a disciplined practitioner of listening for God to speak, as Elijah and Abraham did. You will need to find the discipline that works for you, but here is a suggested model to get you started.

Seven ways and times to pray

1. Read the Gospel passage of your assigned day as a Sunday night prayer the week before you read. It is sometimes helpful to think of prayer as a conversation. The key to being a good conversationalist is to be a good listener. If we take time to listen to God's word in the Gospel, to pray over it, to let it sink into our hearts, we will be better able to enter into the conversation. We will be more confident and clearer about "saying our piece" when our time to speak comes.

   ◆ Some people pray with the Scriptures by reading an entire passage and letting the words and images float in their minds and hearts. Then they read the passage again,

and again they pause to allow the words
and images to hover within them. Then
they read a third time, or perhaps several
more times, letting the words of the
Scripture sink in more deeply each time.

- Others read the Scripture very, very slowly.
  Almost a word at a time, lingering over
  each bit, spending minutes with each
  phrase or sentence.

- Others read the story a few times, each
  time imagining themselves as a different
  character in the story or an observer just
  off to the side of the story. They imagine
  their own actions and reactions as the
  story unfolds.

- Whatever method you use, it will
  strengthen your abilities as a lector to
  spend time in prayer with Scripture,
  especially the Gospel passage for the
  Sunday you are scheduled to read.

2. Another way to spend time praying with
   Scripture is to read your assigned reading as
   your morning prayer every day the week
   before you read. This will root the Scripture
   in your heart and in your head. You will
   begin to breathe the words and phrases in
   and out. You will carry them with you
   throughout the day. Your reading won't just
   be words on the page. They will be a living
   part of you. They will be your spirit, given to
   the community. They will be the word of

God, but they will also be your words, words
from your heart.

3. Similarly, you can pray the psalm that will be
sung on your assigned Sunday as your
evening prayer the week before as another
way to pray with the Scriptures.

4. Communication is a two-way street.
You have to speak. The assembly has to
listen. So pray not just for yourself. Pray for
the Spirit to open the ears of those who will
hear your reading. Pray that they will not
only hear the word, but they will hear the
exact word they need to hear. Pray they will
receive a word of healing, a word of comfort,
a word of salvation. Pray that the word will
take root in their hearts and transform their
lives. Pray that they will recognize the word
they hear as Jesus, the good shepherd. Pray
that they will know his voice and find
intimate communion with Jesus.

5. And do pray for yourself. Pray that you won't
make a mistake, won't be embarrassed, won't
fall on the way to the ambo—all the "Lord
don't let this happen" prayers you need to
pray. Also pray that you will be gentle with
yourself if you *do* make a mistake. Pray for
the grace to move on and not focus on the
error. But mostly pray for the strength to put
aside your own ego. All of us serve as
lectors, at least a little bit, because we like
the attention. We like being in front of
people; we like being noticed. That is natural

and even healthy. But when our need for self-gratification becomes a little too prominent, it can hinder our ministry and it can hinder the proclamation of God's word to the community. So seek to walk humbly before our God, trying as best you can to let the ego rest in the background and the Spirit take center stage.

6. In many parishes the liturgical ministers gather just before the liturgy begins to pray with one another. If that is not the case in your parish, you might suggest starting the practice. Or you could ask several of the other lectors who are there, but not scheduled, to pray with you before Mass begins. Short of that, you can offer a brief prayer with the other lector who is scheduled with you that day.

7. Your final moment of prayer takes place just before you begin to read. Step to the ambo and pray in silence for an extended period. Take a moment to settle yourself and ask for God's Spirit to be upon you. Take lots of time. Thirty seconds seems very brief when you read it here, but standing in front of the assembly it will seem like minutes and minutes. Take your time. Don't rush. Fill yourself with calmness. When the Spirit moves you, begin your proclamation.

**Lord, be on my lips and in my heart,
that I may worthily proclaim your word.**

**O Lord, open my lips, and my mouth shall
declare your praise.**

Create in me a clean heart, O God.

**My mouth and hands shall praise you,
O God.**

**Lord, touch my lips. Place your words
in my mouth.**

**I give thanks to your name for your love
and faithfulness.**

Examples of prayer mantras

Exercise

Create a prayer "place" and a prayer "time" for the coming week. Every day that week, go to the same place, at the same time, and try one of the methods of prayer discussed in this chapter. Or simply sit in silence. Commit to at least five minutes of prayer time each day.

STEP 2

Read Scripture

The Sunday lectionary is divided into three cycles: A, B, and C. These cycles are based upon the first three Gospels—Matthew, Mark, and Luke. These are called the "synoptic" Gospels, which means to have the same view. Although they each have their own unique characteristics, these three Gospels view the story of Jesus' life and ministry in much the same way. The Gospel of John has a significantly different story line and style of writing.

Matthew

Matthew is read in Cycle A of the liturgical cycle. The Gospel of Matthew, though it is placed first in our Bibles, is not the earliest Gospel. It may have been written well after 70 AD, although no one knows for sure. Matthew is the most Jewish of the Gospels, presenting Jesus as the rabbi of rabbis. Matthew emphasizes the demands of Christian discipleship and the coming of the kingdom of God as evidenced by the death and resurrection of Jesus. Matthew uses quite a bit of material that is found in the Gospel of Mark and also bases some of his information on a lost source that scholars refer to as "Q."

Mark/John

The Gospel of Mark, which is read in Cycle B, is the earliest Gospel, probably written just before or just after 70 AD. While Matthew was writing for a "Jewish" Christian audience, Mark wrote for the gentile Christians who were living in Rome at the time. Mark is usually more concerned with the actions of Jesus rather than his words. Mark wants to show that Jesus is the Son of God through the exercise of Jesus' divine power more than by his theological statements. Nevertheless, the Jesus in Mark's Gospel is the most *human* of any of the Gospels, and Mark shows us traits of frustration, questioning, doubt, and sentimentality we are likely to recognize in ourselves.

Several Sundays in the summer of Cycle B are given over to the Bread of Life discourses from the Gospel of John. John's Gospel is also read during the third, fourth, and fifth Sundays of Lent in Cycle A. These Lenten readings are the stories of the Samaritan woman at the well, the man born blind, and the raising of Lazarus. The Cycle A readings may be read every year, especially in places where there are catechumens. John is the latest and longest Gospel, probably completed between 90 and 100 AD. Scholars suspect this Gospel may have been written by more than one person. Perhaps much of it was composed by John, the son of Zebedee and brother of James, and some material may have been reworked and added to by his disciples. John's Gospel is said to be the most "theological" with the concept of

Jesus as the Son of God more clearly developed than in the synoptic Gospels.

Luke

Luke was a gentile who was not an eyewitness to the ministry of Jesus. The principal source for his writings was Mark. Other sources would have been collections of sayings and traditions, both written and oral. He probably drew on some of the same sources that Matthew did. Luke's Gospel is often referred to as the social justice Gospel because of his strong concern for the weak and disadvantaged in his society at that time. Luke also had a forward-looking view of the role of women in the church and the world. The date of the Gospel is often placed between 80 and 90 AD.

The weekday lectionary has two cycles

While the Sunday lectionary is arranged on a three-year cycle, the weekday lectionary follows a two-year cycle. There are only two readings on weekdays, with the Gospel always being the second. The Gospel follows a single, continuous cycle. The first reading alternates every other year between the Year 1 cycle and the Year 2 cycle.

Eight-step preparation plan

1. Read the entire Gospel of that year's cycle every Advent. The liturgical year begins

every year on the first Sunday of Advent. With the liturgical year, we also begin a new Gospel. Throughout the year, we hear the story of Jesus from the point of view of one of the evangelists. Part of your task as a lector is to help the assembly understand the point the evangelist is trying to make. The better you know the tone and feeling of each Gospel, the better you will understand how your reading helps prepare the assembly to hear the point of the Gospel. Read the Gospel of John in the summer of Cycle B.

Read the Gospel from a Bible that you are not afraid to mark up. Highlight or underline words, phrases, and sentences that you find interesting. Don't rush your reading. If something strikes you, linger with it. Don't feel as if you have to finish the entire Gospel in one or two sittings. Take your time and really focus on what you are reading.

2. The Sunday lectionary includes three readings and a psalm for each week. When preparing for a Sunday, read the Gospel first. The Gospel, along with the homily, is the climax of the Liturgy of the Word. The other readings lead up to it.

3. Next read the first reading. This is usually a reading from the Old Testament, and it usually foreshadows the Gospel in some way. (There are exceptions to this. For example, the first reading in the Easter season is taken from the Acts of the Apostles.)

4. It is also important to familiarize yourself with the psalm since it is part of the Liturgy of the Word. In some parishes, a seasonal psalm is substituted for the assigned psalm. Find out the practice in your parish and familiarize yourself with the psalm that will be sung on the day you read.

5. Then read the second reading. The second reading, from the New Testament and often from one of the letters attributed to St. Paul, is a semi-continuous (read from beginning to end) reading that was chosen to roughly flow along in the order set down in the New Testament. It was not usually chosen with the other readings in mind. Sometimes it seems to fit amazingly well and other times it seems dissonant and a little out of place. Read all three readings (and the psalm) even though you will only be proclaiming one. It is important to know how your reading relates to the rest of the Liturgy of the Word.

6. It helps to read the readings in context. Read the readings from the week before and the week after. That will give you a sense of the flow of the Liturgy of the Word from week to week and how your reading fits into that flow.

7. Next read enough of the passages in the Bible before and after your passage so that you get a sense of the original story being told. If you are the second reader, you may

want to read the entire letter from which the reading is taken.

8. Finally, having done all this preparation, read your assigned reading.

Exercise

Commit to becoming more knowledgeable about the Bible. Each time you are scheduled to read, try to learn one new thing about the author(s) of the book you are reading from or something about the composition of the book itself. For example, can you give a one- or two-sentence description of the author(s)? Do you know about what year or what century the book was written? What language was the book originally written in? Do you know who the intended audience was? Is the named author really the author? (For example, some of the letters attributed to St. Paul were not written by him.) All this information and more can usually be found in the introduction to the book in your Bible.

Find the most important phrase in your reading

All of this reading and praying has a purpose. It is your goal to find in your reading the single most important phrase that you will emphasize with the way you read. In the reading from 1 Kings that was referred to in the Introduction, there is one key thing the assembly needs to understand. Because of the dramatic elements of the reading, it is easy for a lector to focus on the wind, or the fire, or the earthquake. It is tempting to play up the elements that at first seem most engaging and captivating. Or perhaps the lector might recognize Elijah's fear and read in a way that highlights that aspect of the reading. Or, in the worst case, the lector might give no emphasis at all to the reading, proclaiming each line with equal weight, allowing the words to wash across the assembly in a gray fog.

What is important in the 1 Kings reading is the understanding that Elijah found God in the sheer silence. The entire reading is about that single idea. As the bearer of God's word, as a sculptor of the silence, your challenge is to proclaim the reading in such a way that the assembly clearly hears what the most important point of the reading is. If you do all of your initial preparation, and then follow this four-point model, you will be able to discern the most important phrase to emphasize in any reading.

How to discern
the most important phrase

1. As you do your preparatory reading, look for the key element in the assigned Gospel for your Sunday. That will give you a clue as to the most important phrase in your reading.

   ♦ You can discern the key element in the Gospel from a careful reading (in context) of the Gospel story itself.

   ♦ You can also read the Gospel in the context of the liturgical year to find a clue about the key element. For instance, the Gospel for Christmas Day is the beginning of the Gospel of John ("In the beginning was the Word, / and the Word was with God, / and the Word was God."). There are several possible ways to interpret that Gospel, but its assignment to Christmas Day tells us it has to do with the incarnation of the Lord. If you are assigned as the first reader for that day, you might keep in mind the key notion of "incarnate word" as you try to discern the most important phrase in the Isaiah reading for that day.

- ◆ Oftentimes it is possible to ask the homilist what key element of the Gospel will be preached on that Sunday. Perhaps it doesn't seem as though that would be very easy to do. However, many homilists begin preparing their homilies long before most lectors begin preparing their readings. A voice mail message or an e-mail to whoever is scheduled to preach on the Sunday you read might be a simple way to find out what the key element of the Gospel is that week.

- ◆ Another process that is helpful is to meet with a small faith-sharing group to break open the readings. The insights of the group can help you discern the most important phrase.

2. Once you've done the work of finding the key element of the Gospel, go back and read your reading again. Keeping in mind that key element, underline phrases that jump out at you in your reading. Underline words and phrases that are interesting, disturbing, or moving. In other words, you are looking for the phrase that really sticks out for you—the one that wants you to pay special attention to it.

3. As you are reading and as you are discerning the phrase on which you will focus, pray for guidance. Ask the Spirit to lead you to find

the words that most need to be proclaimed that Sunday. There is no absolutely right or wrong phrase to choose. Choose the phrase that seems most important. Many readings will have only one key phrase. Many others will have more than one. If you are unable to discern one clear phrase, spend some time in prayer, and turn it over to the Holy Spirit to guide you.

4. Oftentimes there is no one phrase that must be chosen as the most important one. There might be several within a given reading. One isn't necessarily more correct than the other. However, it is very important that you choose only *one* point to emphasize. It is often too difficult to emphasize more than one phrase in the short readings we are usually assigned. And even if you do an excellent job emphasizing more than one phrase, the assembly will have difficulty knowing where you are focusing your reading. So choose only *the most important phrase* to emphasize.

Once you know what the most important phrase is, underline it and set it off with double slash marks. Now comes the fun part. Practice reading in such a way that your most important phrase really stands out. Build the intensity, rhythm, and passion up to the point of your first two slash marks. Then come to a complete, cold stop. Look straight up at the assembly. Read your phrase slowly, clearly, and powerfully from memory. Stop at your next two slash marks. And then finish the reading. For example, in the 1 Kings reading, you might begin the reading in a normal voice at a somewhat leisurely pace. As the wind goes by, increase your pace and intensity. When the fire happens, get a little louder and a little more insistent. By the time the earthquake happens, your voice should sound like an earthquake.

Exercise

Do the work of finding the most important phrase in your reading at least a week before you are scheduled to read. Memorize your phrase and use it as a prayer mantra throughout the week. Alternatively, discern what the most important phrase in the Gospel is, and use that as a prayer mantra.

Another useful exercise is to see if you can discern the most important phrase when other lectors read. What did they do that made the phrase stand out?

STEP 4

Find the emotion

Most readings have a primary emotion. Emotions are strong feelings such as anger, joy, fear, or love. Many times, the key phrase that you have selected will be a guide to discerning the emotion of the readings. Read over the passage several times, focusing on the key phrase, and find the emotion you think is strongest in the reading.

Some readings will have several emotions. With lots of practice, you may be able to express more than one emotion in your reading. However, most readings are so brief, it is best to discern what the primary emotion is and to try to proclaim the reading while giving emphasis to that primary emotion.

Some readings are less emotional than others, and it may be difficult to discern much emotion at all. Other readings may have so many emotions, it may be difficult to focus on the primary one. If you are having difficulty, look at the psalm of the day. The psalms were chosen to help the assembly focus on the spirit and mood of the readings, and they can help you do the same thing. Use the psalm as an aid to help you discern the emotion. See the list of emotions for examples.

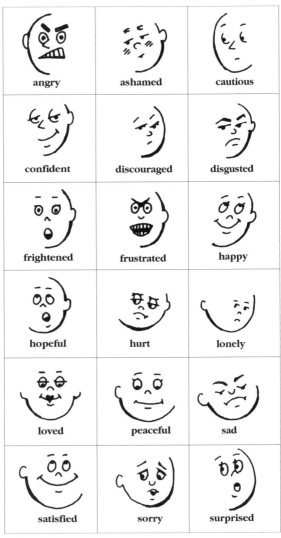

Examples of emotions

Once you have decided what the primary emotion of your reading is, you might want to write the emotion in the margin of the page of your Bible or lectionary. That will serve as a reminder to you as you practice your reading.

For example, the primary emotion in the story of Elijah in 1 Kings might be fear. You can almost feel the fear in him when he tells the angel that all the prophets have been killed and he is next on the list.

Now take a minute to focus on that emotion. Think back to times when you've felt that emotion. Try to remember a time all the way back to your childhood when you felt that emotion most strongly. Let the emotion build up within you. If it is a negative emotion, it might be a little difficult. In that case just do what you can do, and don't go any further than you need to in order to capture the feeling of the reading.

Using the Elijah story as an example again, when have you ever felt deathly afraid? Think especially of times when you were young and you were afraid. Recall the feeling, and let it build up in you until you have some understanding of how Elijah feels in the story.

As you practice your reading, focus on the key emotion and recall that feeling. As you read and practice the proclamation, let that feeling flow through you. Read in such a way that the feeling comes through in your voice, your facial expression, and your body posture.

In our example of Elijah and feeling fearful, pay attention to your posture, how your muscles feel, what your face looks like, and what your breathing is like when you are afraid. Try to recapture those same physical feelings and characteristics as you practice the reading.

Exercise

Make it your goal to generally become more aware of your emotions. Pay attention to your emotions for an entire day. Set an alarm or tie a string around your finger or put your watch on the wrong wrist to remind yourself to do an emotions check throughout the day. Pay attention to the tension or lack of tension in your arms, back, legs, and face. Identify your feeling as pleasant or unpleasant. Try tracking your emotions on a work day versus a weekend day. Are there differences?

STEP 5

Practice

Next comes the actual practice. It seem almost unnecessary to remind lectors that they need to practice, and yet, many skip this absolutely crucial step. And many lectors, probably most, do practice, but don't practice effectively. If you follow these six suggestions, you will be much more effective both in your practice sessions and in your proclamation.

1. Read silently.

- ◆ Read the passage silently several times. As you read, try to get a sense for the pace and flow of the reading. Try to understand the meaning of the reading more deeply. Focus on your most important phrase and how you are going to communicate that to the assembly.

- ◆ Underline the verbs in the reading. When we read, we tend to emphasize the nouns and adjectives. However, the reading will be much more powerful if you emphasize the verbs.

- ◆ Make a list of any unfamiliar words as you read. Look up the definitions of any words

you do not know. Use a Bible dictionary
for place names or names of characters
you do not recognize.

♦ Look up pronunciations of words you do
not know.

2. Memorize.

There are at least two lines you should memorize
in your reading—the first line and the most
important phrase.

As you begin the reading, look straight out at
the assembly (or the imagined assembly during
practice). Say where the reading is taken from,
and, without looking down, deliver the first line
of the reading. So, for example, if you are the first
reader on the Nineteenth Sunday in Ordinary
Time, Cycle A, you would recite the following,
completely from memory, without looking down:

A reading from the first Book of Kings
At the mountain of God, Horeb, Elijah
came to a cave where he took shelter.

Then, when you came to the point you had
identified as the most important phrase, you
would look up, deliver the line from memory,
looking straight at the assembly, pause, and then
go on with the reading. And so, on the 19th
Sunday, Cycle A, you might choose the following
line to be proclaimed by heart:

(pause) … and after the fire there was a
tiny whispering sound. *(Pause.)*
["a sound of sheer silence" in the NRSV]

Memorization sounds scary if you aren't used to doing it, but it gets much easier with practice. If you are not confident enough to memorize two lines at first (the opening line and the most important phrase), then focus on memorizing just the most important phrase. After you grow more comfortable with that, try doing the first line of the reading from memory also.

The reason for doing these lines from memory may be somewhat obvious to you. When you first begin the reading, the assembly is already looking at you. They are already communicating with you through their eye contact. If you immediately break eye contact and look down, they will also look down or look away. You don't want that to happen. And with the most important phrase, you want to create as much connection with the assembly as possible so they will better be able to hear that line. That means you have to have full eye contact with them when you proclaim that line.

Now you may be wondering, If a little memorization is good, is more memorization better? As a rule of thumb, it is usually better not to memorize the entire reading. To proclaim an entire reading from memory takes a great deal of skill and practice. For some people, it can be quite difficult to proclaim a reading from memory without having it sound like it is being done from memory. In other words, too often what is going on in the assembly—instead of listening to the word of God—is a sense of admiration and awe at the "skill" of the lector who has memorized all the words. If memorizing the text calls attention to you and not to the word, it is better not to do it by heart.

3. Read out loud.

- ◆ Always practice the reading out loud, and, as much as possible, try to simulate the conditions under which you will actually be doing the reading. So, for example, if you have ready access to the worship space, practice in the worship space. At the very least, be sure you practice the reading standing up in the largest room in your house.

- ◆ Read the reading several times, trying different sounds with your voice. Emphasize the underlined verbs and try different ways of emphasizing your most important phrase.

- ◆ Practice on at least two different days before your scheduled reading date. Practice at least three times each day for a total of at least six times. Six times is the bare minimum for well-trained lectors who know how to practice efficiently. It is not a magic cutoff number. Practice as many times as you need to in order to proclaim the reading to the best of your ability.

4. Get feedback.

Getting feedback during your practice sessions is essential. There are several ways to get feedback, and the more of them you use, the better you will be as a lector. The most basic feedback mechanism is to practice in front of a mirror. Look at your facial expressions, your body language, and your physical presence. Does your nonverbal behavior convey the emotion of the reading? How do you look when you are nervous? Will you appear to be nervous when you are doing your proclamation? What do you want to look like? Practice in front of the mirror until your body "remembers" the correct look.

Another very simple feedback method is to tape-record yourself. Most of us have a distorted concept of how we actually sound. A tape recording provides a quick, accurate method of feedback.

Even better, practice in front of a video camera if you can. In my experience, lectors improve dramatically after only a single viewing of themselves on video. Even if you can't practice with a video all the time, it is a good idea to have a friend or someone in the parish videotape you during a practice session at least once a year.

A little scarier, but very helpful, is to practice in front of somebody. Grab someone in your family, even one of the younger children, and ask them to give you an honest critique. Ask them what they thought the most important phrase was, based on the way you read. If they don't know, you have more work to do.

5. Practice with other lectors.

Of course, some of the best people to give you feedback are other lectors. If you don't have regular training sessions in your parish, you can at least organize a few other lectors to meet with you on occasion for rehearsal sessions. After all, the musicians of the parish practice together regularly. Shouldn't the lectors rehearse together also?

When you gather to rehearse together, it is important that you focus on strengths. It is easy to fall into the trap of being overly critical. Then you or the other lectors begin to feel as if you are not really good enough to do this ministry. You become overly worried about making mistakes, and the reading itself becomes an exercise in avoiding pitfalls rather than a passionate proclamation of God's saving word. If you stick to the following suggestions, you will avoid that mistake.

The first volunteer proclaims a reading he or she will be doing on an upcoming Sunday. When the reading is complete, the volunteer *must* say one thing he or she liked about how he or she read. This is crucial. We *all* know what we are not good at. We often have trouble saying what we are good at. So don't let yourself or anyone else off the hook with phrases like "I really didn't like how I read" or "I really liked what St. Paul had to say in this reading." The lector must say one clear thing that was good about his or her own technique in the proclamation.

Until that statement is made, there should be no critiquing comments from the group, either positive or negative. Sometimes there will be long silences while the lector struggles to come up with something positive to say. That's okay. Remember, no comments from the group about the reading until the lector's own *positive* comment is made first. This is important because we have to help each other learn how to give ourselves positive reinforcement.

Once the lector's own positive comment is made, the rest of the group can then contribute their own comments about what they *liked*. At this point, no negative comments should be allowed.

Once all the positive comments have been made, the lector would then name *one* thing that he or she believes needs strengthening. There may be more, but there will be other rehearsals. The point is to focus on strengths and not become overburdened with the things that are not so strong. One thing at a time is plenty to work on. At this point there should be no critiquing from the group. Every once in a while, a lector will misidentify what needs the most work. For example, she may think she needs to work on her pacing when what really needs much more work is her projection. In that case, if there is a leader of your group (the pastor, the liturgist, a lector coordinator), he or she might gently suggest to the lector that she might also work on projecting more forcefully.

The lector then reads a second time, focusing on the one element in need of strengthening. The group then gives feedback about the level of improvement. Be honest. If the weak spot was not any better the second time around, gently point that out and give suggestions for what the lector might try to do better.

Then repeat the process with each of the other lectors. Obviously this process is meant for smaller gatherings of lectors since it can be quite time-consuming. Lectors from the same Mass time might gather separately. Or lectors for a season of the year such as Advent or Lent might gather for this kind of rehearsal to keep the numbers manageable.

6. Practice in front of a mentor.

The best way to improve in the long run is to seek out someone you think is an excellent reader. Ask that person for advice, and ask for honest critiques about your reading style. People sometimes don't ask for a critique because they are afraid of what they might hear. Our American culture tells us we should be able to figure out how to improve on our own. If we can't do it by ourselves, there must be something wrong with us. The truth is, however, an effective way to improve is to seek advice from those who have more skill and talent. Seek out someone you respect and ask if that person would be willing to evaluate you.

The most effective way to work with your mentor might be to schedule a rehearsal (in the church, if possible) *after* you have done all the preparation and practice you think you need in order to do your best possible job. Then your mentor can evaluate you at what you think is your best and help you improve from there. Also ask your mentor to be present on the Sunday you read.

After your mentor has heard you read, ask him or her to tell you what you did well. Discover where your strengths are and continue to build on them.

Then ask the mentor, "What can I do to improve?" It might be hard to hear where you are weak, but don't shy away from asking.

If you have a difficult time accepting negative critiques (as most of us do), you might ask your mentor to agree to give you only positive, but honest, feedback the first time he or she hears you read. Then, in later sessions, ask what you can do to improve for next time.

Exercise

As soon as you get your lector schedule, put your assigned days into your calendar. While you have your calendar out, also schedule appointments with yourself (and your mentor?) for practice times.

Use eye contact

U sing strong, consistent eye contact is one of the most effective ways to involve the assembly in the proclamation. Unfortunately many lectors use little or no eye contact. Some lectors get too nervous to look up. Others have not practiced their reading enough to be able to take their eyes off the text even briefly. And others simply forget how important it is. The general rule is, the more eye contact the better. However there are six key moments when you should be certain you are making eye contact.

1. The first crucial moment is just before you say "A reading from the book/letter of …." At the moment just before you are about to begin, look at the assembly for an extended moment, locking onto their eyes and letting them lock onto yours.

2. The second moment flows directly from the first. As discussed in the practice session, memorize the first line of the reading itself. Then deliver "A reading from the book/letter of …" and the first line of the reading without looking down at the text. Use your eye contact to keep the assembly involved in

the reading from the very beginning. Note that even though you haven't yet looked down at your text, you have already established two distinct moments of eye contact. The first is a look that makes a connection and gets the attention of the assembly. The second is one that leads the assembly in participating in the reading itself. It may look like one instance of eye contact to the casual observer, but be aware of the two distinct purposes and moments involved.

3. Make eye contact on words and phrases that deliver the key emotion of the reading. In Step 4, we discussed how to find the key emotion. If the primary emotion is joy, for example, be sure to make eye contact on words and phrases that sound joyful.

4. Make eye contact on foreshadowing phrases. Foreshadowing is a technique authors use to give little clues about what is to come later in a story. Look for words and phrases that give an indication about the meaning of the most important phrase of your reading. Also look for words and phrases that foreshadow the main point of the Gospel. Then attempt to make eye contact at those points in the reading.

5. If you don't do it anywhere else, make eye contact on the most important phrase that you have selected from the reading. Linger with it. Drill the phrase into the assembly with your eyes. Be sure everyone in the

room has a sense you are looking directly at them when you proclaim the phrase.

6. Finally, make direct eye contact when you say "The Word of the Lord" at the end of the reading.

Some people are naturally better at making eye contact than others. If you have difficulty making eye contact, add more repetitions to your practice schedule. Practice makes eye contact easier. Even the most inexperienced lector can make eye contact a few times in a reading if he or she practices enough.

The new lectionary layout makes eye contact easier. It is printed in sense lines so even if you lose your place for a moment, it is easier to know where to pick up the beginning of the next line. Also, the new lectionary uses larger print, making it easier for lectors to look up from the text and find their place again. And the new lectionary has eliminated almost all page turns so you don't have to worry about knowing what's on the back of what you are reading.

Some lectors use an index card to follow along the text. That helps them keep their place as they look up. It works just as well to follow along with your fingers to keep your place.

Exercise

For an entire day, practice making eye contact when you speak to someone. Become conscious of how many times you look away from the other person's eyes when you are speaking or when he or she is speaking. If you are speaking with a group of people, be conscious of making eye contact with each person. Be aware of making eye contact with people you pass by while walking. Make eye contact with checkers and lunch counter servers.

> **Key emotion = fear**

Go outside and stand on the mountain before the Lord.

A reading from the first Book of Kings   **19:9a,11–13a**

At the mountain of God, Horeb,
> **Elijah <u>came</u> to a cave where he <u>took</u> shelter.**
Then the LORD <u>said</u> to him,
> **"<u>Go</u> outside and <u>stand</u> on the mountain before the LORD;**
> **the LORD will be <u>passing</u> by."**
A strong and heavy wind was <u>rending</u> the mountains
> **and <u>crushing</u> rocks before the LORD—**
> **but the LORD <u>was not</u> in the wind.**
After the wind there <u>was</u> an earthquake—
> **but the LORD <u>was not</u> in the earthquake.**
After the earthquake there <u>was</u> fire—
> **but the LORD <u>was not</u> in the fire.**
// After the fire there <u>was</u> a tiny whispering sound.   *// Most important phrase*
When he <u>heard</u> this,
> **Elijah <u>hid</u> his face in his cloak**
> **and <u>went</u> and <u>stood</u> at the entrance of the cave.**

> **The word of the Lord.**

Example of a page from the lectionary with the verbs marked, key emotion noted, and the most important phrase identified.

Project

If there is one thing that almost every lector needs to focus on, it is projection. If more lectors would project more effectively, many of the other weaknesses they have would fade away or become less significant. Although improving one's projection is perhaps the single most important thing a lector can do, it is also perhaps the most difficult technique to teach. Many of us have a deceptive sense of how much we are projecting. I once worked with a somewhat quiet lector whom I knew had the ability to project well, but nothing I tried got her to use her full voice. Finally she admitted she was holding back because she had always been told how loud she was and she was afraid of blasting the ears of the assembly. She really thought she was lifting the roof off the church, when, if fact, she was barely audible. It is very easy to deceive ourselves about how we sound.

Projection is very important because of all the things it does to help the assembly participate in the reading. Projecting well does four important things for your proclamation:

1. Good projection usually increases the volume of the reading so people can hear better. If

parishioners have a single common objection about lectors, it is that they can't be heard. The first responsibility of the lector is to make the word heard. Projecting your voice will ensure that, at the very minimum, the people in the assembly will hear the words.

2. But projecting is not just about being louder. True projection also adds color and depth to our voices. Someone who is projecting well can speak quite softly—if the style of the reading calls for it—and still be heard. For example, in the Elijah story from 1 Kings, the phrase "a sound of sheer silence" would be read in a very soft voice. Projecting, while reading softly, will allow you to be heard. Using effective projection gives you a lot more tools to add drama and interest to the reading.

3. Projecting well also provides power and confidence to the proclamation. The assembly is more likely to be engaged and more likely to trust what you are saying if you project because you will sound as though you know what you are talking about.

4. Finally, good projection allows you to read longer without having to take a breath because you are using your breath more efficiently. This means you can break phrases where they are supposed to be broken instead of having to break them because you run out of air.

For all these reasons, simply turning up the sound system will not work as effectively as projecting well. A higher sound level all by itself will not add color and depth and confidence to your voice. It will simply amplify your bad proclamation habits. Your best strategy is to imagine that you have no microphone and proclaim the reading as though you are trying to convince the people in the back pew of the importance of what you are saying.

To project effectively, you have to use your diaphragm muscle. The diaphragm is located just under the lungs. It is a big muscle that you use when breathing deeply to fill your lungs with more air.

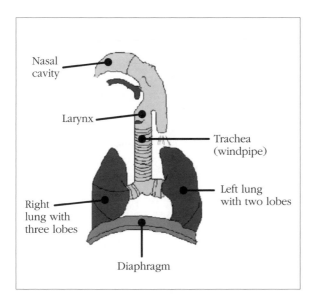

Nasal cavity

Larynx

Trachea (windpipe)

Left lung with two lobes

Right lung with three lobes

Diaphragm

When you inhale, you can inhale in one of two ways: You can inhale in such a way that you are only taking in a little air. Think of how a soldier would stand at attention with stomach in and chest puffed out. That is the *wrong* way to inhale. The second way to inhale is to imagine you are a child pretending to be Santa Claus. Using your diaphragm, you pull air down as far as possible into your lungs, pushing your stomach out to make it as "fat" as possible.

There are also two ways to exhale: The first is to use your upper chest muscles and your throat muscle to push air out of your lungs and through your mouth and nose. This is the *wrong* way to exhale. The second way is to use your abdomen muscles and your "fat" stomach to push the air from the bottom of your lungs through your throat, mouth, and nose.

When you breathe in deeply and exhale by using the force of your abdomen—and you make vocal sounds while doing so—you are projecting. For some people, it can be very, very hard to even know for sure if they are breathing the right way or the wrong way. To test yourself, try this exercise:

1. Lie on the floor.

2. Put a book on your stomach.

3. Breathe in such a way that the book goes up and down.

4. If the book isn't moving or isn't moving very much, you are not breathing the right way. Keep practicing until you get the correct

breathing rhythm. Once you get it, remember
the way your body feels and moves. You
must breathe this way when you are reading.

Now try another exercise. Stand up, and place
your hand on your stomach. Then shout "ha"
three times fast (HA, HA, HA). You should feel the
same muscles moving as when you were lying on
the floor, and you should feel your hand moving
in each time you expel breath with the word
"ha." Your hand should move farther underneath
your rib cage, toward your spine, as though you
were trying to squeeze your stomach in to be able
to buckle a very tight belt.

Once you have that exercise mastered, try this
next step. Take your reading and imagine each
syllable as a separate *sentence.* Using your
projection technique, shout each syllable-sentence
of the first couple of lines of your reading. So,
taking our 1 Kings reading as an example, you
would imagine it to be written this way:

At. The. Moun. Tain. Of. God. Hor. Eb.
E. Li. Jah. Came. To. A. Cave. Where. He.
Took. Shel. Ter.

Place your hand on your stomach, contract your
abdomen muscle hard, and explode each
"sentence" out of your mouth in the same way you
shouted "HA, HA, HA." Do that a few times until
each "sentence" seems to fill the room with sound.
Slowly smooth out the flow into a more natural
sound and rhythm. But even when you are
speaking "normally," you should still feel your
hand on your stomach moving in as you speak.

This technique will get easier and easier the more you practice. Once you are doing it well, you will be able to fill most rooms with the sound of your voice. Always rely on your projection to carry your sound for you. Do not rely on the microphone. The microphone is an aid, but it should not do all the work for you. If you do not project and instead let the mic carry your voice, your proclamation will be robbed of color, depth, and confidence.

Exercise

Practice projecting in ordinary conversations. You don't have to speak more loudly than normal. Remember projection isn't necessarily about being louder. Just place your hand on your stomach and practice speaking while projecting from your diaphragm. Try putting your watch on the wrong wrist as a reminder to project while speaking on the phone or contributing to a meeting.

Vary your pace

Pacing is an important factor that often gets overlooked. Many times a lector begins to read at a fast clip and continues at the same speed throughout the entire reading. This is most often due to nervousness rather than to a considered reflection on what kind of pace the reading calls for.

Many trainers will simply tell lectors to read more slowly. If a lector is not able to discern the different paces needed within a reading, generally a slower pace is indeed better than a faster pace. However, with a little effort, almost any lector can learn to "change gears" within a reading, getting either faster or slower as the text calls for.

The first step is to identify the different *speeds* of the sections of your reading: fast, medium, slow. Some parts of some texts do call for a very fast, almost incomprehensible pace. For example, think of Exodus 14:15—15:1, which we read at the Easter Vigil. In this reading, Moses leads the Israelites through the Red Sea. The Egyptians follow in hot pursuit. Moses stretches his hand out over the sea again, and the waters flow back on the Egyptians. This reading can start out slowly, almost as a stately march as the Israelites, in stunned awe at the power of God, pass between the walls of water. The pace picks up as the Egyptians follow, the sound of your voice beginning to pick up the rhythm of the rolling chariots and galloping horses. Finally, as the water falls back on the Egyptians, you push yourself to the limit, trying to match the speed and panic of the Egyptians as they begin to realize what is happening and try desperately to escape their watery tomb. And then everything comes to a stop. A dead stop. In the silence of mortal awe, as the Israelites contemplate the awesome power of their God—perhaps fully realizing for the first time just who has called them out of Egypt—you slowly, carefully, frightfully, deliver the news that "not a single one of them escaped."

Identify the different *rhythms* of the sections of your reading. Using the Exodus reading, you can identify possible marching rhythms, staccato rhythms, galloping rhythms, walking rhythms, melodic rhythms, and dancing rhythms. There is almost *no* rhythm as the Egyptians are drowning, but instead a chaotic mix of tempos. Let your imagination roam as you try to imagine the possible rhythms in your reading.

Sometimes just reading the text to yourself doesn't lend itself to discovering different paces. Try different, even ridiculous paces when you practice. Try the opposite pace of what you think should logically be the right pace. Movies do this all the time. The monster chases the hero in what should be a frantically paced scene but is instead shot in slow motion to heighten the suspense.

What would it sound like if you read the scene of the Egyptians chasing the Israelites at an almost glacially slow pace? Maybe it would sound silly, or maybe it would sound powerful. You won't know until you try.

Finally, be sure your most important phrase is not overlooked in your pacing. Usually, you can make a dramatic shift—from fast to slow, for example—when you get to the most important phrase. Remember to use your double slash marks. Start the reading at a slow or medium pace. Build the pace up to a somewhat fast speed, and come to a dead halt at the slash marks. Then read the most important phrase slowly and clearly. At the next set of slash marks, pick up the pace a bit and keep it steady through the rest of the reading. This is one way to use pacing to set off your most important phrase. Many times it will work, but sometimes it won't. Experiment. Try different speeds and combinations of speeds. Listen to your tape, and get other feedback. Decide what kind of pacing is most effective in setting off your most important phrase.

The Israelites had marched on dry land through the midst of the sea.

A reading from the Book of Exodus   14:15—15:1

The LORD said to Moses, "Why are you crying out to me?
Tell the Israelites to go forward.
And you, lift up your staff and, with hand outstretched over the sea,

split the sea in two,
that the Israelites may pass through it on dry land ...."

Begin with a slow, stately pace.

The angel of God, who had been leading Israel's camp,
   now moved and went around behind them.
The column of cloud also, leaving the front,
   took up its place behind them,
      so that it came between the camp of the Egyptians
      and that of Israel.
But the cloud now became dark, and thus the night passed
   without the rival camps coming any closer together
      all night long.
Then Moses stretched out his hand over the sea,
   and the LORD swept the sea
      with a strong east wind throughout the night
      and so turned it into dry land.
When the water was thus divided,
   the Israelites marched into the midst of the sea
      on dry land,
   with the water like a wall to their right and
      to their left.
The Egyptians followed in pursuit;
   all Pharaoh's horses and chariots and charioteers went
      after them
   right into the midst of the sea.
In the night watch just before dawn *Begin to pick up the pace.*
   the LORD cast through the column of the fiery cloud
   upon the Egyptian force a glance that threw it into
      a panic;
   and he so clogged their chariot wheels
   that they could hardly drive. *Increase pace.*

With that the Egyptians sounded the retreat before Israel,
　　because the LORD was fighting for them against
　　　　the Egyptians.

Then the LORD told Moses, "Stretch out your hand
　　over the sea,
　　that the water may flow back
　　　upon the Egyptians,
　　upon their chariots and
　　　their charioteers."

Even faster, panicky pace. Match speed to galloping horses.

So Moses stretched out his hand over the sea,
　　and at dawn the sea flowed back to its normal depth.
The Egyptians were fleeing head on toward the sea,
　　when the LORD hurled them into its midst.
As the water flowed back,
　　it covered the chariots and the charioteers of
　　　Pharaoh's whole army
　　which had followed the Israelites into the sea. //
<u>Not a single one of them escaped.</u> //
But the Israelites had marched
　　　on dry land
　　through the midst of the sea,

Read slowly. Full eye contact. Pause.

Finish the reading with a moderate, even pace.

　　with the water like a wall to their right and
　　　to their left ....

The word of the Lord.

// = Dead stop. Long pause.

Exercise

Use your favorite Dr. Seuss book as a way to train yourself in pacing. Most Seuss stories have obvious fast and slow parts. If you have young children or grandchildren, practice reading the story to them with as many different paces as you can. Even if you don't have children, you can still have fun practicing silly and exaggerated paces (both slow and fast) with the storybook. Your goal is to see what you are capable of. Play with the story, and read it several times in several different ways.

STEP 9

Vary your style

Literary style

You don't have to be a lector for very long before you realize that the Scriptures contain a wide variety of styles. Does your style of proclamation change with the style of the reading? For convenience, it is easiest to think of the Scriptures as falling into one of four broad categories. These are:

> Stories
> Prophesies
> News
> Poetry

Identify which of the following readings are poetry, prophesy, news, or a story:

Isaiah 52:7–10
(Christmas Day Cycle A)

How beautiful upon the mountains
 are the feet of him who brings glad tidings,
announcing peace, bearing good news,
 announcing salvation, and saying to Zion,
 "Your God is King!"

Hark! Your sentinels raise a cry,
    together they shout for joy,
for they see directly, before their eyes,
    the LORD restoring Zion.
Break out together in song,
    O ruins of Jerusalem!
For the LORD comforts his people,
    he redeems Jerusalem.
The LORD has bared his holy arm
    in the sight of all the nations;
all the ends of the earth will behold
    the salvation of our God.

1 Samuel 16:1b,6–7,10–13a
(4th Sunday of Lent, Cycle A)

The LORD said to Samuel:
    "Fill your horn with oil, and be on your way.
I am sending you to Jesse of Bethlehem,
    for I have chosen my king from among his sons."

As Jesse and his sons came to the sacrifice,
    Samuel looked at Eliab and thought,
    "Surely the LORD's anointed is here before him."
But the LORD said to Samuel:
    "Do not judge from his appearance or from his lofty
        stature,
    because I have rejected him.
Not as man sees does God see,
    because man sees the appearance
    but the LORD looks into the heart."

In the same way Jesse presented seven sons before Samuel,
   but Samuel said to Jesse,
      "The LORD has not chosen any one of these."
Then Samuel asked Jesse,
      "Are these all the sons you have?"
Jesse replied,
      "There is still the youngest, who is tending the sheep."
Samuel said to Jesse,
      "Send for him;
      we will not begin the sacrificial banquet until he arrives
         here."
Jesse sent and had the young man brought to them.
He was ruddy, a youth handsome to behold
   and making a splendid appearance.
The LORD said,
      "There—anoint him, for this is the one!"
Then Samuel, with the horn of oil in hand,
      anointed David in the presence of his brothers;
      and from that day on, the spirit of the LORD rushed upon
         David.

Acts of the Apostles 14:21–27
(5th Sunday of Easter, Cycle C)

After Paul and Barnabas had proclaimed the good news
   to that city
   and made a considerable number of disciples,
      they returned to Lystra and to Iconium and to Antioch.
They strengthened the spirits of the disciples
   and exhorted them to persevere in the faith, saying,
      "It is necessary for us to undergo many hardships
      to enter the kingdom of God."

They appointed elders for them in each church and,
>   with prayer and fasting, commended them to the Lord
>   in whom they had put their faith.

Then they traveled through Pisidia and reached Pamphylia.
After proclaiming the word at Perga they went down to Attalia.
From there they sailed to Antioch,
>   where they had been commended to the grace of God
>   for the work they had now accomplished.

And when they arrived, they called the church together
>   and reported what God had done with them
>   and how he had opened the door of faith to the Gentiles.

Ezekiel 2:2–5
(14th Sunday in Ordinary Time, Cycle B)

As the LORD spoke to me, the spirit entered into me
>   and set me on my feet,
>   and I heard the one who was speaking say to me:
>   Son of man, I am sending you to the Israelites,
>   rebels who have rebelled against me;
>   they and their ancestors have revolted against me to this
>   very day.
Hard of face and obstinate of heart
>   are they to whom I am sending you.
But you shall say to them: Thus says the LORD God!
And whether they heed or resist—for they are a rebellious
>   house—
>   they shall know that a prophet has been among them.

Answers: Ezekiel 2:2–5 is a prophesy; Acts 14:21–27 is
news; Isaiah 52:7–10 is poetry; 1 Samuel 16:1b,6–7,10–13a
is a story.

60

Stories are the big epics that Hollywood tends to make movies out of. The story of the Israelites crossing the Red Sea, the great flood, and the creation story are a few examples of some of the story Scriptures. To find a style, think of a grandfather who, at every gathering, recounts the family history or some past great adventure that a long-dead ancestor embarked on. That's the style you would strive for if you are assigned one of the storytelling readings.

Prophesies are readings that usually call for a little fire and brimstone. Some people hear the word "prophesy" and think "future telling" or "fortune telling." That's not quite what we mean by prophesy in the Scriptures. A prophesy isn't really about telling how things are going to be in the future. It's more about telling how things *should* be in the future. A prophet is someone who is usually calling for a reform of the status quo. And that almost always means a prophet is an unpopular person. People didn't like being told they had to change in the ancient days of the Scriptures any better than they do now. It takes some courage to proclaim the prophetic readings in your own assembly. You are, in effect, telling your fellow parishioners to shape up or ship out. You need to read the prophetic readings with a style that is strong and confident, but always keep a sense of personal humility right below your fiery delivery.

News reports are the kinds of readings that often turn up in the letters from St. Paul. These readings are something like messages from the home office. Paul or other newsy writers are communicating good news to communities they are close to and want to stay in touch with. Sometimes these readings are helpful hints to live by. Sometimes they are updates or clarifications in theological thinking. To get the right style, you should think of yourself as a modern-day newscaster with an important message to deliver.

The Scriptures are filled with poetry. The most obvious poetic "reading" we hear each week is the psalm. However, lectors are also asked to read poetry when the lectionary cites passages from Isaiah, Daniel, Revelation, and other books that rely heavily on symbol and metaphor. There is no single poetic style. It is important to understand the mood of the reading and to understand something of what the symbols and metaphors mean. Try to match your proclamation style to the emotion of the poetry. Try not to read in a singsongy voice that too easily dominates much poetic reading.

Author's style

Another aspect of style is the personal style of the author. Some people are basically happy. Some are basically melancholy. Your challenge is to discern the style of the author you are reading and catch something of his or her personal style in your proclamation. For instance, St. Paul can be said to have a very intense style that can often flare up in outbursts of anger. But that same intensity and passion can also manifest itself in quite stirring protestations of faithfulness and love. St. Peter, on the other hand, seems to be a simpler, more laid-back kind of personality. Yet he exhibits a deep and quiet faith that can awe us at times. How would your style be different if you were reading from one of Paul's letters as compared to one of Peter's letters?

Time of year

The season of the year should also have some impact on your style. The contrast between Lent and Easter is the most obvious. Lent might call for a more somber, perhaps prophetic style calling the community to repentance and the catechumens to conversion. Easter would lend itself to a joyful style of proclamation.

Advent would call for a sense of anticipation. The readings in the Christmas season call out for a style that exudes wonder and awe.

Winter ordinary time could take on a style of exhortation and preparation. In many places, the outdoor season is cold and barren at this time of year. The "indoor" church season is a time of preparing those catechumens who are about to become members of the Elect on the first Sunday of Lent. The Ordinary Time Sundays from the feast of the Body and Blood of Christ to Christ the King Sunday are quite varied. Break them up into blocks to see if you can discern an overall style for sections within this long season. The end of the season, from late October through November, takes on a sense of the coming end times, and the style of proclamation might focus on anticipation and even anxiety.

Style of the assembly

The assembly in which you will proclaim the readings will also influence your style. The Saturday 5 P.M. community is going to respond best to a different style than the 11 A.M. Sunday community. The Church of the Most Holy Nosebleed is going to best hear one style of reading while the Community of Contemporary Hipsters will best relate to another style. Be sure you know your community and what style they will most clearly understand.

Exercise

Identify your personal style. Are you flamboyant or low-key? Are you a storyteller or a news reporter? Schedule a day in the next week in which you will try to emulate a style that is different. For instance, if you are usually low-key, try wearing a flower to work. If you are usually bubbly and chatty, try being quiet and a little "shy" for the day. Your goal is to grow more comfortable using styles that are foreign to you.

The Well-Dressed Lector

Things lectors worry about

Nervousness

Even with all the best preparation in the world, lectors still worry. Someone once identified public speaking as the most compelling phobia that humans suffer from. And lectors have to deal with that fear every time they approach the ambo. No matter how many years some of us have been reading, we still get nervous. Most of us will never completely overcome our nervousness, but there are a few things we can do to minimize it.

Prayer/mantra. Lectors must be people of prayer. If you have an active prayer life, God will remind you daily that you are not in charge. God has called us to this ministry and it is God's job to get us through it. It can sometimes be quite soothing to remind God of that fact. The Scriptures are filled with people who didn't want to speak, but God shoved them out on stage anyway. Moses, Jeremiah, Jonah, and others whom God called all tried to shirk their call to proclaim the Good News. But God got them through it. And God will get you through it.

It helps to have a mantra to help calm your nerves. A mantra is a short prayer that you match to your breathing. So, for example, you might pray "Lord Jesus Christ" as you inhale deeply and slowly. Then pray, "have mercy on me your servant" as you exhale slowly. Repeat the prayer and the breathing over and over until you are calm. You can choose any phrase you like for a mantra. It can be from the Scriptures or a favorite childhood prayer or one you make up. The key is to keep it very short and to match it to your deep breathing. (See page 11 for other examples of prayer mantras.)

Practice and preparation. Adequate practice goes a long way toward calming jangly nerves. If you find you are extraordinarily nervous before you read, try adding to your practice time. A good lector with lots of experience should rehearse the reading at least six times before Sunday arrives. A lector with less experience should double that, so there are at least twelve practice sessions before Sunday. If you are rehearsing your reading a dozen times, and you are still unduly nervous, try adding even more practice sessions. Also try to practice in the actual space in which you will be reading. Visualize yourself on Sunday morning approaching the ambo confidently and strongly. Visualize yourself standing before the assembly. Imagine they are anxiously awaiting the good news you have to give them. Visualize yourself proclaiming the word with power as the Holy Spirit flows through you.

On the day you are to read, be sure you are well prepared. Allow yourself enough time in the morning to get ready for church so you won't be rushed. If you are not a morning person, pick out what you will wear the night before. Set out your purse or wallet, sunglasses, keys, and anything else you might be prone to misplace. Arrive at the church thirty minutes early. Check to see that the lectionary is in the right place and the correct Sunday is marked with the ribbon. Note any line breaks in the lectionary text that might be different from your practice text. Repeat out loud any difficult words. Repeat your mantra a few times, and remember you are God's instrument. Then station yourself at one of the entrances and greet your fellow parishioners as they begin to arrive. Try to focus on them, and not on your own nervousness.

Look the part. Even with a saintly prayer life and a preparation regimen that would rival a space shuttle launch, you may be at least a little bit nervous. The trick is not to show it. Remember to smile. For many people, a nervous look is often interpreted as an angry look. A smile makes you look calm and confident. Walk with purpose, even before the liturgy begins, but especially when walking in procession and approaching the ambo. Keep your shoulders back and straight. Walk at a dignified pace. Think of yourself as a ship that is sailing through the assembly. No sudden starts, stops, or turns. Everything moves smoothly and deliberately. When it is time to approach the ambo, move with the same shiplike deliberateness. If you need to don reading glasses, it is best to do so before you go to the ambo. If you have trouble negotiating steps, either use the handicap ramp or ask another lector or one of the acolytes to assist you. It is much preferable to have a brother or sister help you to the ambo than it is to go it alone and stumble on the way there. Once at the ambo, take a moment to get your bearings. Breathe deeply. Repeat your mantra. Then wait. Do not rush into the start of the reading. Wait for a long silence thirty to sixty seconds—until the assembly is absolutely still. Wait confidently and cooly, even though you may be shaking inside. Keep breathing. Keep repeating your mantra. Begin when the assembly is ready.

When you are finished with your reading, do not rush away from the ambo. Remember you are a ship. It takes a moment for a ship to change course. Let the end of the reading ring in the ears of the assembly for a moment, then turn gracefully and return to your place. Once seated, do not lean over to those next to you and comment on how poorly (or well!) you thought you did. If someone makes a comment to you, simple pat them on the hand by way of acknowledgment, and focus on the action of the liturgy. Once the liturgy is over, if someone offers you a compliment, accept it graciously with a smile and a thank you. Don't respond with comments about how poorly you did.

Your goal in acting confident is not to pretend to be something you are not, and it is not to somehow fool the assembly into thinking you are better than you are. The goal is to train your "confidence muscle." Weight trainers lift just a little more weight than they are comfortable with in order to build strength. To build your confidence, you need to act just a little more confident than you think you are. With enough practice and repetition, you will build up your strength. Soon you really will be more confident—and less nervous.

Mispronouncing a word or blowing a line

Slipping up in the middle of a reading happens to every lector sometime. It is part of the human condition. The best way to deal with that is to accept it as a fact of life and not let it dominate your thoughts.

Nevertheless there are some steps you can take to make it happen less often and to minimize the damage when it does happen. It should be obvious that lectors would look up words they don't know. Should be, but often it doesn't happen. Make a hard-and-fast rule for yourself. Never read a word in public that you are not *absolutely certain* of. You should be certain of the meaning as well as the pronunciation. This includes the names of people and places. Know who and where they are. Know how to pronounce them. Keep a couple of dictionaries nearby: a good English dictionary and a good Bible dictionary.

Once you know the meanings and pronunciations of all the words in your reading, practice the reading until you have it down perfectly. Practicing until you are confident using the unfamiliar words is the best way to guard against mispronouncing them. Also practice difficult turns of phrase or sentences that contain tongue twisters.

Even with all this preparation, it will still happen that you will stumble on a word or miss a line. When it happens, *do not apologize.* Apologizing only draws attention to your mistake. Don't let a small mistake turn into a larger one. Don't let one small slip rattle you and cause you to lose your concentration. Just calmly move on to the next line as though nothing happened. Usually it is best not to return to the blown line. However, if the line you have skipped or mangled is crucial to the understanding of the reading, simply return to the beginning of the sentence and proceed from there. There is no need to compound the mistake with a phrase such as, "Let's try that again." Stick to the lectionary text, and don't add in your own commentary.

Being too dramatic

Many lectors fear they are being too dramatic. Don't worry. You're not. It is very rare to find a lector who is actually over the top. The opposite case—not being dramatic enough—is by far the more common problem.

Part of the issue is what we understand "dramatic" to mean. Some people hear the word "drama," and they think of playacting. Mass is not playacting. The thinking goes, "Mass is real, and so therefore it cannot be a drama." This is too simple an understanding of the word "drama" and it is not helpful in understanding the role of the lector. The original Greek word *drâma* means a consequential act. The liturgy is certainly a consequential act, and it is, in a sense, a sacred drama. When we notice something in the liturgy we think of as "too dramatic," it is usually something that is not being done very well. It is not *good* drama.

Think of how this works in your own experience of drama. When you have experienced a professional production, perhaps a Broadway play in New York or something of that caliber, were you sitting through the entire play thinking to yourself, "these actors are really dramatic"? Or were you caught up in the story? Did you think the characters were real? Did you *believe* the play and players?

Compare that with your experience of a high school production. Even the very best high school plays will leave parents and friends commenting on how the actors were *almost* good enough for the professional stage. Most high school plays fall well short of that high praise. In any case, we usually don't really get caught up in a high school play so completely that we *believe* the characters are real and the story is real. We think we are watching a bunch of high school kids, some of whom have talent, and all of whom have worked really hard and deserve a big hand at the end for their efforts.

The professional production is drama. The high school production isn't. Yet it is in the high school production that we are aware of the "acting." We think of the players as "actors" and not as the characters they are attempting to portray. Most of the young actors come off as "hammy" and "too dramatic." In fact, they are not dramatic enough. That is, they haven't mastered the art of drama the way their professional elders have. The pros are usually the true dramatists, using the skills of the theatrical arts to convince us that the story they are telling is true.

Lectors need to spend more time striving to become more dramatic—that is, mastering the art of theater—so their proclamation will be convincing and compelling.

What to do if you are asked to read at the last minute

T his happens to every lector. Usually it's because another lector did not show up when scheduled. About five minutes before Mass, someone taps you on the shoulder and whispers, "Can you read today?" Invariably, the reading you are asked to do is a long one, filled with unpronounceable words. Yet, you feel compelled to offer your service to the community. Next time it happens to you, follow these seven steps.

1. **Don't worry.** That may sound difficult. You would have been able to do a better job if you'd been able to practice, but that isn't an option. Take a deep breath, pray your mantra, and trust in the Spirit.

2. **Scan the reading.** Look for any difficult words, and ask the presider or another lector how to pronounce them. Whisper them out loud to yourself a few times. Try to pronounce them confidently when you

actually do the proclamation, even if you are still unsure of the pronunciation. If you don't know how the word is pronounced, chances are very few people in the assembly will know either.

3. **Read the reading out loud at least once.** There is almost always time to get in at least one read-through. If need be, ask the presider if the procession can be delayed for sixty seconds or so while you go through the reading. If you cannot read the text in full voice, at least whisper it.

4. **Practice your first line in your head.** If you can, try to get the first line or the first few words of the first line into your head before the procession starts. Repeat the line over and over to yourself as you are processing. This is not ideal, of course. Ideally you would be singing the opening song. But this is not an ideal situation, and your immediate goal is to make the proclamation as good as possible under the circumstances.

5. **Pause before reading.** When you go to the ambo, you would ideally pause for a brief moment of prayer before beginning to read. Take an even *longer* moment to make a brief prayer and then go over the opening line in your head again. Take all the time you need to feel confident. Do not rush. No one is in any hurry, and the assembly will wait for you. Be slow, deliberate, and confident.

6. **Don't worry about eye contact.** The new lectionary is written in sense lines, which makes eye contact much easier than it used to be. Some lectors can make quite a bit of eye contact even when doing a reading cold because of the way the text is broken. However, in this situation, the most important thing is to proclaim the text clearly and smoothly. Make significant eye contact just before you begin to read. Make eye contact, if you can, during the opening line that you have been rehearsing in your head. Make eye contact at the end of the reading. Anything else you are able to do *comfortably* is a bonus.

7. **Don't apologize.** If someone thanks you or compliments you on your reading after the liturgy, be gracious. There is no need to explain how much better you could have done if you'd been able to practice or to comment on how badly you think you did. If you did the best you were able to under the circumstances, that is what is being acknowledged.

Frequently asked questions

1. Where should the lectors be in the opening procession?

The order of procession varies from parish to parish. The most usual order is for the lector carrying the lectionary to be second-to-last in line, right in front of the presider. The other lector is third-to-last. When the procession reaches its destination, the process for placing the book on the ambo also varies from place to place. Usually all the ministers in the procession either bow to the altar or genuflect. In most cases, the lector carrying the Word would neither bow nor genuflect. In some parishes, the lector carrying the lectionary bows his or her head but does not "dip" the lectionary. That is also acceptable. If the custom in your parish is for the ministers to genuflect, and if it is important in your community that all the ministers *do* genuflect, it is best to place the book on the ambo, return to the foot of the altar, and then genuflect.

2. How high should the book be held?

The higher the better. At a minimum, the bottom of the lectionary should be at about eyebrow level. Stretch your comfort level and raise it a bit higher than that. Ideally, the lector would extend his or her arms as much as possible in order to create a true sense of procession with the book.

Imagine that you are proclaiming the word with the very first step of your procession. How would you make the proclamation nonverbally? How would you let the assembly know, before you ever reach the ambo, that the word of God is among them? Use your body, the rhythm of your walking, and the way you carry the book to make that proclamation.

3. Should the book be held during the reading?

The new lectionaries have almost made this a moot point. If you are using one of the new Sunday lectionaries, it is impossible to hold them for long because of their size. If for some reason you have a smaller lectionary and you wish to hold the book as you read, that is probably a good thing to do. It works just as well, however, to leave the book on the ambo as you read.

It should go without saying that the lector should always read from a bound lectionary. Every symbol we use at Mass should be worthy and dignified. It should not look temporary or disposable. So no paperback lectionaries, workbooks, missallettes or looseleaf papers. Always read from a worthy book.

4. Is it okay for lectors to use hand gestures during the reading?

Hand gestures are tricky to pull off. The first thing to ask is why a lector would want to add in a gesture. Will the gesture significantly add to the proclamation of the reading? Will it help the assembly to better understand and "hear" God's word that day? Too often, a gesture is simply distracting. It can call attention to itself and to the lector and not really help the proclamation. But on occasion, used sparingly and well, a simple gesture can emphasize the most important point of the reading and add an important element to the proclamation.

Here are some general guidelines for adding gestures.

- If you are at all unsure about using the gesture, don't.

- If you have never before used a gesture in your reading, start out using only one.

- Practice, practice, practice in front of a mirror. Make sure the gesture is natural, confident, and smooth.

- Know your assembly. For some assemblies, no matter how good you are and how natural the gesture is, it won't work.

♦ Generally, the larger and more festive the liturgy, the more appropriate a gesture would be. So in most cases a gesture would work better at the Easter Vigil than at a summer time weekday Mass.

5. Should the lector lift up the book at the end when saying, "The word of the Lord"?

There is no need to raise the book at the conclusion of the reading. The lectionary *is* in a sense the word of God. But the sounds that come out of the lector's mouth are also the word of God. And the action of the Spirit in the hearts of the assembly as they hear is also the word of God. And as the word becomes incarnate in the assembly, the assembly itself also becomes the word. So when the lector says, "The Word of the Lord" at the conclusion, it includes all those senses of the word. Elevating the book places too much emphasis on only one of the meanings.

6. Where should the lectors sit?

The ideal would be for the lectors to sit in the midst of the assembly. However, this also varies from parish to parish so check with your parish leaders. When the lector comes from the assembly to proclaim the reading, it creates a clear sense that the ministries flow from the assembly.

7. Should the lectionary be carried out at the end of Mass?

There isn't an absolute rule, but generally, what is carried in the opening procession is carried out at the end of Mass.

8. How should lectors dress?

Lectors should dress up. Proclaiming the word of God is a sacred ministry, and lectors should dress as though they have a sacred calling. Casual dress gives an air of the ministry being casual. What "dressing up" means varies from community to community and even within communities. So even though the ideal is to dress up, lectors need to be careful not to criticize each other about how they dress. What is casual for one person may be dressy for another.

9. How many lectors are required on Sunday?

There would ordinarily be one lector for each reading. If lectors do all the preparation required for *one* reading, it would be quite difficult and time-consuming to prepare two. Even if a lector was willing to put in the work required to prepare two readings, why wouldn't a second lector be scheduled to do one of the readings? In a secular drama, actors usually play only one major role, not two. The sacred drama of the liturgy calls for a full complement of ministers. Some parishes will have difficulty recruiting enough lectors at some of the lower participation liturgies (stereotypically, the Saturday evening liturgy or the very early Sunday morning liturgy). Nevertheless, there would usually be an ongoing effort to increase the overall participation at these liturgies and to recruit more lectors and other liturgical ministers. A lector should do more than one reading only in emergency and compromise situations. The scheduling process should never be such that having only one reader is a goal. So, for example, if John Jones is the only reader scheduled Saturday 5 P.M. Mass, his name should appear twice simply to reinforce the idea that he is acting in a double capacity.

10. Would a third lector be required for the psalm and a fourth for the intercessions? What about the announcements?

The ministry of the lector is not to "read stuff at the microphone." The ministry of the lector is to proclaim the word of God. So the lector would not ordinarily read the intercessions or announcements. Although this does happen in many parishes, it is not the ideal. It is a habit we have fallen into and that we should extract ourselves from. The usual minister for leading the intercessions and making announcements is the deacon. If there is no deacon, the ministries of the deacon fall either to the cantor, the presider, or another minister, but not to the lector.

The psalm is the word of God, but it is not a reading. It is a song and, at least on Sunday, it would ordinarily be sung.

11. Can a lector also serve as a communion minster or other liturgical minister?

This would also be a case in which a lector would double up only in an emergency or compromise situation. If a lector takes his or her ministry seriously, that person is lector even at times when he or she is not reading—just as a priest is a priest even when he is not presiding at Mass. As a lector, how do you make the word present when you are not scheduled to read? How do you make the word present when the Liturgy of the Word has ended and the Liturgy of the Eucharist has begun? More elementally, what does it say about our seriousness about fulfilling the mandate of the Second Vatican Council to expand the liturgical ministries as broadly as possible, if a few people are serving in two or three ministries? If you really feel called to be a communion minister or an usher or a choir member, resign from your role as lector and serve in the ministry you are most called to. If you can't decide, serve in one for a year and then switch to another for a year. If you serve at one of the "low participation" liturgies and for the time being you and the other ministers are unable to recruit more help, then try your best at least not to serve in two ministries at the same liturgy. So, for example, you might be a lector on the Twenty-eighth Sunday of Ordinary

Time and a communion minister on the Twenty-ninth Sunday, but you would avoid doing both ministries on both Sundays.

12. What are the differences among translations of Scripture?

None of Scripture was originally written in English. Most of the New Testament was written in ancient Greek and much of the Old Testament was written in Hebrew. Translations of Scripture began to occur almost as soon as it was written. Several modern translations are excellent. The translations Catholics might most frequently encounter are the New American Bible, Revised Standard Version, New Revised Standard Version, Jerusalem Bible, and Contemporary English Version (used in the *Lectionary for Masses with Children*). Any of these translations may be used in parishes for prayer, study, and catechesis. In parishes in the United States, only the NAB may be used in the liturgy. In parishes in Canada, only the NRSV may be used in the liturgy.

The most widely used translation among Protestants is perhaps the King James Version. The KJV is unrivaled for its masterful use of the English language. However, it dates from the 1600s, and more accurate translations have superseded it for use in scholarly, theological work.

BIBLIOGRAPHY

Bretzke, James T. *Consecrated Phrases: A Latin Theological Dictionary: Latin Expressions Commonly Found in Theological Writings*. Collegeville, Minn.: Liturgical Press, 1998.

Harpercollins Bible Dictionary. Rev. ed. Edited by Paul J. Achtemeier, Roger S. Boraas, and Michael Fishbane. San Francisco: Harper San Francisco, 1996.

Liturgy of the Word: Readings, Psalms and Antiphons for Sundays, Holy Days and Weekdays. Schiller Park, Ill.: World Library Publications, annual.

McKenzie, John L. *Dictionary of the Bible*. New York: MacMillan Publishing Company, 1995.

Rosser, Aelred R. *Guide for Lectors*. Basics of Ministry Series. Chicago: Liturgical Training Publications, 1998.

Staudacher, Joseph M. "Lector's Guide to Biblical Pronunciations." *Our Sunday Visitor* (1990).

Wallace, James A. *Ministry of Lectors*. Collegeville, Minn.: Liturgical Press, 1985.

Workbook for Lectors and Gospel Readers. Chicago: Liturgy Training Publications, annual.

WEBSITES

Lector (Catholic Encyclopedia)
http://www.knight.org/advent/cathen/09111a.htm

New American Bible
http://www.nccbuscc.org/nab/bible/index.htm

Readings and psalms for the month
http://www.nccbuscc.org/nab/index.htm

Frequently asked questions about the New
  American Bible
http://www.nccbuscc.org/nab/faq.htm

Audio Bible (uses the King James Version but may be
useful for some pronunciations)
http://www.audiobible.com/bible/bible.html